YOUR KNOWLEDGE HAS VALUE

Comprehensive and Comparative Review of Covid-19 detection using various deep learning techniques

Hardik Modi
Dev Patel
Sagarkumar Patel
Vishal Tank

Bibliographic information published by the German National Library:

The German National Library lists this publication in the National Bibliography; detailed bibliographic data are available on the Internet at http://dnb.dnb.de.

ISBN: 9783346985989
This book is also available as an ebook.

© GRIN Publishing GmbH
Trappentreustraße 1
80339 München

Print and binding: Books on Demand GmbH, Norderstedt, Germany
Printed on acid-free paper from responsible sources.

The present work has been carefully prepared. Nevertheless, authors and publishers do not incur liability for the correctness of information, notes, links and advice as well as any printing errors.

GRIN web shop: https://www.grin.com/document/1433128

Comprehensive and Comparative Review of Covid-19 detection using various deep learning techniques

Hardik Modi

Department of Electronics & Communication Engineering, Chandubhai S Patel Institute of Technology, Charotar University of Science and Technology, Changa, Anand, Gujarat, India.

---***---

Abstract

The coronavirus disease 2019 (COVID-19), as designated by the World Health Organization, is causing a pandemic that will affect the entire world. The severe acute respiratory syndrome coronavirus 2 (SARS-CoV-2) virus, which is the source of COVID-19, was first identified in late December 2019 in Wuhan, China. Within a few months, the virus had spread in various countries across the world. Because COVID-19 affects millions of individuals worldwide, it has turned into a global health emergency. The most typical symptoms of COVID-19 virus are fever, a dry cough, and gastrointestinal issues. Being extremely contagious, the illness readily spreads to persons in close touch with those who are infected. Contact tracking is a good way to stop the virus from spreading, according to us. Convolutional neural networks (CNNs) in particular have achieved successful outcomes in the categorization and analysis of medical image data using artificial intelligence (AI) approaches. This survey and research proposes a deep CNN architecture for the diagnosis of COVID-19 based on the classification of chest X-ray and CT-Scan images. This review article explains how to use a database of X-ray and CT-Scan images from patients with common bacterial pneumonia to automatically diagnose coronavirus infection., proven Covid-19 infection, and common cases. The study's objective was to assess the value of COVID-19 acquisition. Globally speaking, the number of infected cases increases dramatically in the COVID-19 scenario. Because of this, medical professionals and infected patients made the crucial option to quickly embrace various medical facilities.

Keywords: Deep learning, Feature extraction, Image classification, Convolution Neural networks, Artificial Neural Networks.

Table of content

1. Introduction

The first instance of the new coronavirus COVID-19 was found in Wuhan, a Chinese city. The World Health Organization (WHO) acknowledged that this virus could result in respiratory illnesses through coughs, the flu, and pneumonia in December 2019. Since that time, the virus has started to spread throughout China and many other nations. First, connections with seafood and live animal markets were reported among COVID-19 new affected individuals in central Wuhan, China, illustrating the animal-to-human transmission of the disease. Following that, an increase in the number of affected individuals who were not in contact with live animals caused the transmission of the disease from person to person. The medical relevance of COVID-19 can be shown in a number of symptoms such as moderate fever, nausea, and cough. One of the categories under IEEE 2021 is MERS or SARS. Access to and download of this publication are free, as are the rights to full text mining, data re-use, and analysis of COVID-19. SARS is also a respiratory illness caused by the (SARS-CoV) virus, which was first identified in 2003 in Southern China and spread to many other parts of the world. A few symptoms of COVID-19's complicated medical presentation include coughing, moderate fever, and nausea. The second wave of the current coronavirus disease 2019 (COVID-19) pandemic appears to be far more hazardous than the first wave, which is extremely regrettable. In the second wave of the severe acute respiratory syndrome coronavirus 2, India is one of the most impacted nations (SARS-CoV-2). Due to the fact that they have not recovered from the initial wave, the USA and Brazil are also two vulnerable nations. On January 24, 2023, India had a total of 44,682,015 sick persons and 530,735 fatalities, and that number is rising [1]. Given their proximity and the fact that the Indian strain of SARS-CoV-2 is more hazardous than the other types, this is upsetting for Bangladesh. All ages can get the virus, which is spreading quickly and can Cause catastrophic sickness. The World Health Organization has estimated that there are roughly 664,097,132 COVID-19 cases shown in Figure 1 [2] and 6,716,108 fatalities worldwide shown in Figure 2 [1] [2].

3

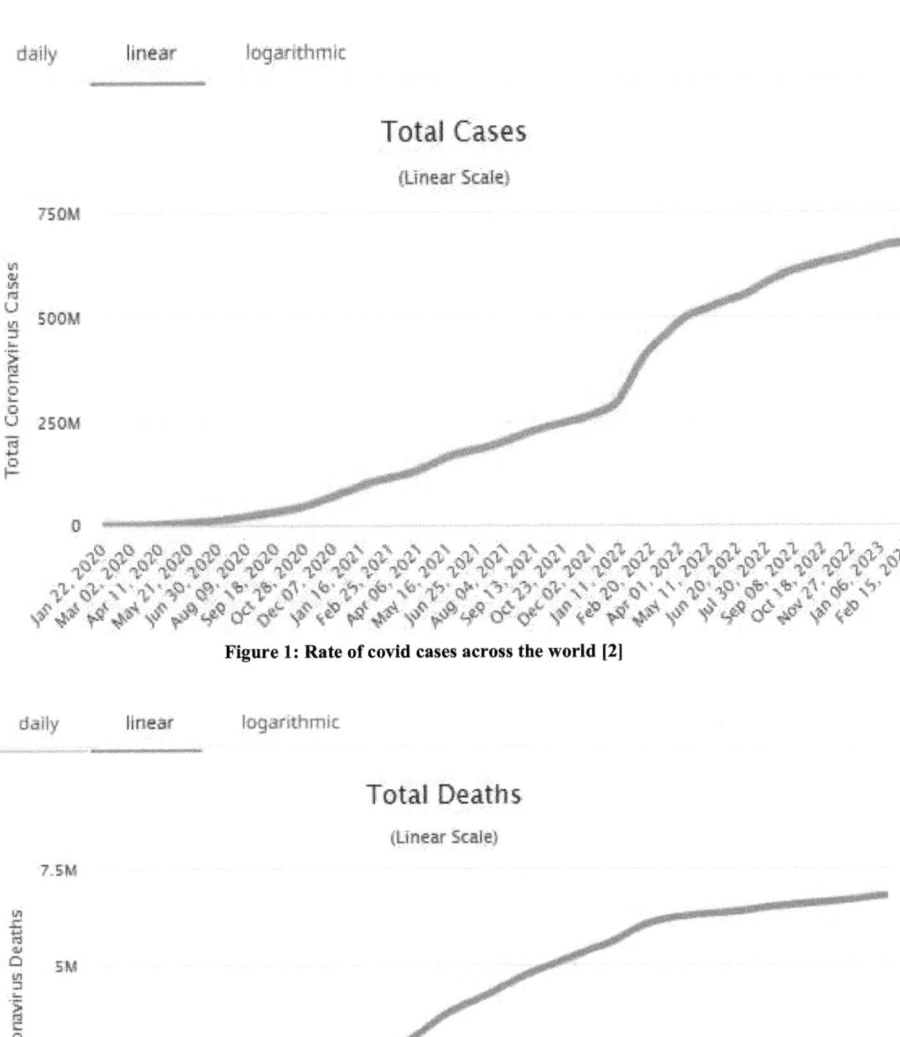

daily   linear   logarithmic

Total Cases
(Linear Scale)

Figure 1: Rate of covid cases across the world [2]

daily   linear   logarithmic

Total Deaths
(Linear Scale)

Figure 2: Rate of covid deaths across the world [2]

4

In most cases, the virus targets the lungs of an infected person, leading to pneumonia. It immediately lowers the oxygen level after that. Since there was no treatment for this virus, the only option before a vaccination is to stop its spread. So yet, tests and tracing is the only available remedy. In medical science, the polymerase chain reaction (PCR) test is frequently used for testing. But because there are so many cases, it is now almost impossible to run enough PCR testing because it is time-consuming and expensive. Therefore, an additional test is necessary to enable fast isolation or quarantine of sick individuals. Some deep learning techniques have been applied to the identification of viruses so far. The outcomes of these deep learning algorithms, however, are insufficient to handle a system for medical diagnostics. The WHO has declared COVID-19 an epidemic, and a sizable percentage of patients must wait for a CT scan image for several hours in the hospital. In addition to overwhelming the medical system, this frustrates patients more and raises the danger of infection from other patients.

An electromagnetic type of penetrating radiation is called X-radiation or X-ray. To produce photographs of the inside intricacies of the body part, these radiations are delivered through the desired human body parts. The interior body sections are depicted in black and white on the X-ray image. One of the earliest and most widely used methods of medical diagnostics is the X-ray. A chest X-ray offers an image of the thoracic cavity, which contains the bones of the spine and chest as well as soft organs like the lungs, blood vessels, and airways. This image is used to diagnose chest-related disorders like pneumonia and other lung ailments. As an alternate diagnosis method for COVID-19 testing, the X-ray imaging technology has many benefits over conventional methods.   These advantages include the low price, the abundance of X-ray facilities, the non-invasiveness, the reduced time commitment, and the affordability of the gadget. Consequently, considering the current crisis in global healthcare, X-ray imaging may be seen as a better option for the widespread, simple, and speedy detection method for a pandemic like COVID-19 [3].

Figure 3 shows a CT-Scan image, and Figure 4 shows an X-Ray image. The height and width of the images in the dataset were initially different from each other. The shapes of the images were fixed in the model.

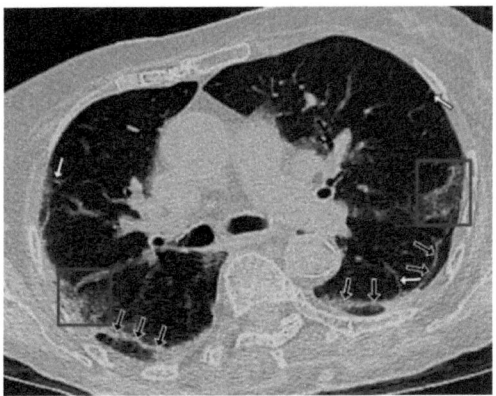

Figure 3: CT-Scan image [4]

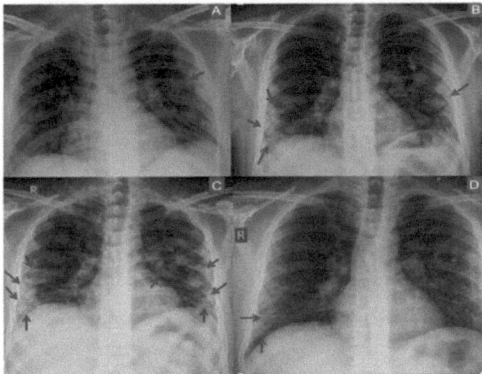

Figure 4: X-Ray image [5]

In light of the current pandemic crisis, there appears to be a connection between the identification of COVID19 cases and the classification and analysis of chest X-ray images. In this study, CNN has been used to create an automatic diagnostic system that determines if a person has COVID-19 or not based on the findings of a chest X-ray analysis. This study's preliminary research has produced encouraging results in terms of accuracy and other performance metrics for timely and affordably diagnosing the condition. In order to increase the COVID-19 X-ray picture classification accuracy, this study applied CNN with additional layers. The CNN structure in neural networks is specifically made to handle tasks involving two-dimensional image processing, while it can also be applied to one- and three-dimensional data. The most popular use for CNN, a form of DNN inspired by the visual system of the human brain, is the analysis of visual imagery.

Additionally, COVID-19 is identified using clinical identification kits. Although pricey, this gadget must be fitted for identification. Modern smartphones are built with lots of sensors and have processing power. The capability of cellphones to record, gather, and store enormous volumes of data in suspected

6

or confirmed COVID-19 situations is one of its primary characteristics. The smartphone may also scan the CT-Scan images of a COVID-19 patient in order to conduct an examination. A comparative analysis of the formation of the lesions can also be obtained by uploading multiple X-Ray and CT-Scan images of the same infected patient to a smartphone. The examination is particularly beneficial in identifying and determining the severity of pneumonia in suspected COVID-19 cases. Acute respiratory syndrome coronavirus 2 (SARSCoV2), which has been linked to more than 44 million cases in India and 619 million worldwide at the time this review study was written, was the primary cause of COVID-19. In fact, the World Health Organization labelled it a pandemic in 2022. Maharashtra became the epicenter with more than 8,125,369 confirmed cases and more than 148,362 fatalities in Maharashtra, India [6]. When the epidemic was at its worst, emergency rooms (EDs) and intensive care units (ICUs) were overcrowded and lacking in resources, which upset medical professionals. The COVID-19 phenotypes include fast deterioration, acute respiratory distress syndrome (ARDS), systemic failure, and death. They also include moderate or insignificant symptoms and repeated recovery [1,3,6].

2. Data Availability

In this review paper most off the authors use combination of dataset which contains more than 3-4 datasets and create their own dataset. Some of the Authors use dataset of covid 19-radiography-database, Cohen's GitHub, COPD Dataset, COVIDx & Clinical datasets [7-10].

3. Search Strategy

In this study, Covid-19 papers were found using reliable databases such as IEEE Xplore, Science Direct, NCBI, Springer Link, Hindawi, ACM, and ArXiv. In addition, a more A comprehensive Google Scholar search is used. The writings are chosen using the terms Corona Virus, COVID-19,Deep Learning, COVID-19 Segmentation, and Detection employing patient symptoms and/or medical images Techniques for machine learning. The most recent choice of papers are completed in Sep 2022 using the stated keywords. depending on the technique for COVID-19 detection and prediction published studies utilizing DL techniques.

4. Pre-Process

Images need to be processed before they can be used for model training and inference. This include, but is not limited to, changes in color, size, and direction. Pre-processing is done to improve the image's quality so we can analyze it more successfully. Through preprocessing, we can get rid of undesired distortions and enhance certain qualities that are crucial for the application we are developing. Those qualities could alter based on the application. For software to work properly and deliver the required results, an image must be preprocessed.

4.1. Gaussian Filtering (GF)

Using the GF approach, a linear smoothing filter used for weight selection based on the structure of the Gaussian function, the input images from the CXR dataset are pre-processed. As a powerful low pass filtering method, the GF technique is applied to the spatial or frequency domain, especially for noise removal. The following denotes the zero means 1-D Gaussian function.

$$g(x)=e-x2/2\sigma2 \qquad (1)$$

The Gaussian functions' width is determined by the parameter used in the Gaussian distribution. When processing images, a smooth filter, a 2D discrete Gaussian function with zero mean, is used. The function is defined as follows.

$$g[i,j]=e-i2+j2/2\sigma2 \qquad (2)$$

4.2. Data augmentation

Making copies of the current data and making minor changes to them is one technique to increase the diversity of the training dataset. The term "data augmentation" applies here.

For instance, that your image classification collection has 20 photos of ducks. You have increased the number of training examples for the "duck" class by doubling them by making duplicates of your duck photos and flipping them horizontally. Other adjustments including rotation, cropping, zooming, and translation are also available. To further increase your stock of original training examples, you can combine the modifications.

4.3. Data Segmentation

Data segmentation is the process of split-up your data into at least two sections, while larger networks with sensitive data may require more divisions. In addition to use cases and information kinds, data should be categorized according to its sensitivity and the amount of access required to access it. A segment-specific set of security restrictions and authentication rules should be established when data has been segmented.

Photographic contrast is improved using a technique known as adaptive histogram equalization (AHE) in computer image processing. The adaptive approach is different from traditional histogram equalization in that it computes many histograms, individually corresponding to a different area of the image, and then uses them to disperse the image's brightness values. Therefore, it is appropriate for strengthening the definition of edges in each area of an image as well as the local contrast. AHE has a leaning to overstate noise in relatively homogeneous areas of an image, though. This is avoided by contrast limited adaptive histogram equalization (CLAHE), a type of adaptive histogram equalization, by restricting the amplification.

4.4. Intensity normalization

An essential stage in the study of brain magnetic resonance images (MRIs) is intensity normalization. Different parameters or scanners would be utilized for scanning various patients or the same subject at various times during MR image acquisition, which might lead to significant intensity differences.

4.5. Data annotation

Data annotation is the process of labelling data in many formats, such as text, images, or videos, so that computers can understand it. Labeled datasets are essential for supervised machine learning since ML models must comprehend input patterns in order to interpret them and generate reliable outputs.

4.6. Histogram

An example of a histogram that visualizes the tonal distribution in a digital image is an image histogram. Each tonal value's number of pixels is plotted. A viewer will be able to rapidly assess the complete tonal distribution of an image by taking a quick look at the histogram for that particular image.

5. Classifier

Any algorithm that organizes data into labelled groups, or categories of information, is a classifier. Spam filters are a straightforward example of a practical system that scans incoming "raw" emails and categorizes them as "spam" or "not-spam." In many types of machine learning, classifiers are a tangible implementation of pattern recognition.

5.1. Sigmoid Activation Function

A real value is entered into the relatively straightforward Sigmoid Activation function, which outputs a probability that is always between 0 and 1. It resembles a 'S' form. It has a set output range, is non-linear, monotonic, and continuously differentiable. The main benefit is that it's easy and useful for classifiers. The function's biggest drawback is that because its output isn't zero-centered, it causes the issue of "vanishing gradients." The gradient updates become excessively divergent as a result. 0 output 1 makes optimization more difficult. In the deep layer of the neural network, that requires very long computation time.

5.2. Rectified Linear Unit (RELU)

The hidden layer of Neural Network uses this activation function, which is the most prevalent. Ma (0, z) max is a deceptively straightforward formula (0, z). Despite its name and outward look, it is not linear and, while performing better than Sigmoid, offers the same advantages.

Its key benefit is that it is less computationally costly than sigmoid and tanh and avoids and corrects the vanishing gradient problem. But there are some drawbacks as well. Occasionally, some gradients can become unstable during training and end up dying. Dead neurons result from this. In other words, the

9

gradient for activations in the region (x0) of RELU will be 0, hence the weights won't change throughout descent. That indicates that the neurons that enter that state will no longer respond to changes in error or input (simply because gradient is 0, nothing changes). As a result, we must choose activation functions carefully and in accordance with business requirements.

5.3. Dense Layer

Each neuron in the simple layer of neurons known as the dense layer receives information from every cell in the layer below it. Based on the results of the convolutional layers, a dense layer is utilized to categories the images. Single neuron in action. Such neurons are found inside a layer in large numbers.

5.4. Softmax

In general, we employ the neural network function at the last layer that computes the probabilities distribution of the event over 'n' distinct events. The function's ability to handle several classes is its key benefit.

5.5. Decision tree

Figure 5 shows an emerging direction is to extract knowledge from neural networks into tree structures, but the trees did not provide a semantically meaningful explanation of the network knowledge. In order to regularize an RNN for better representations, built a decision tree through knowledge distillation to represent the output feature space of an RNN. Vaughan et al. condensed knowledge into an additive model of explanation.

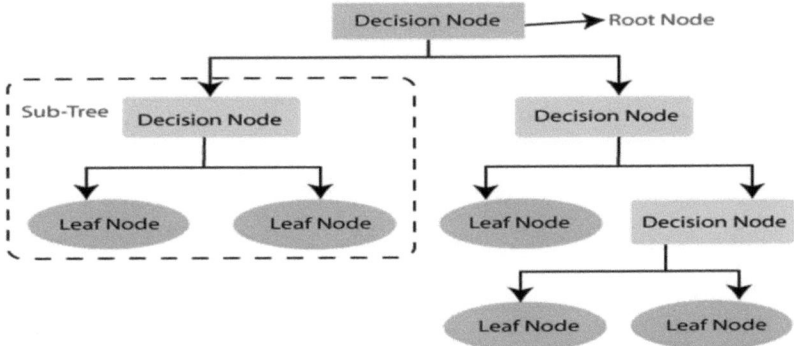

Figure 5: Interpreting CNNs via Decision Trees [11]

6. Evaluation parameters & criteria

A machine learning classification performance evaluation method uses a confusion matrix. It's a type of table that aids in determining how well a classification model performs on a set of test data where the true values are known. Although the phrase "confusion matrix" itself is somewhat straightforward, the vocabulary it refers to can be a little perplexing. Here, we provided a brief explanation of this technique. By contrasting the actual and predicted classifications, the confusion matrix illustrates the accuracy of a classifier. The squares that make up the binary confusion matrix are TP, FP, TN and FN as shown in Figure 6.

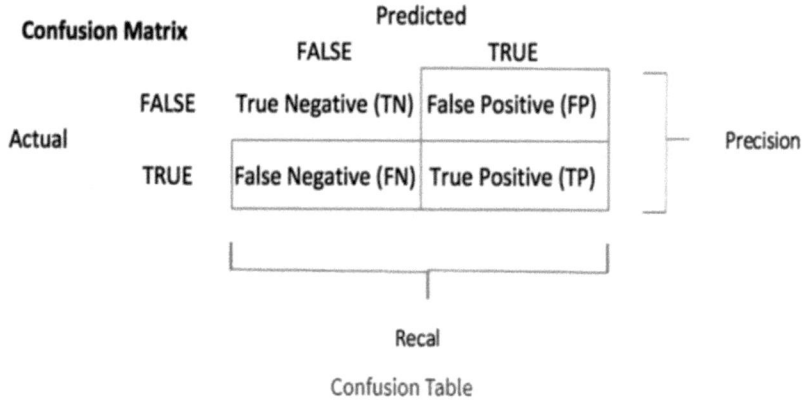

Confusion Table

Figure 6: Confusion Table [12]

TP: True Positive: Predicted values are correctly predicted as actual positive value.

FP: False Positive: values predicted as positive

FN: False Negative: Positive values predicted as negative

TN: True Negative: Predicted values are correctly predicted as an actual negative

Classification accuracy: The percentage of successfully classified images is referred to as the accuracy.

Sensitivity: Examines how well the model recognizes positive events. Given that COVID-19 is a positive category, sensitivity may therefore be used to measure the percentage of times that X-ray images are correctly identified as COVID-19.

Specificity: The percentage of actual negatives that are successfully recognized depends on specificity.

Recall: The percentage of correctly categorized positive subjects to all positive subjects is known as the recall rate. The goal is to raise it as much as you can.

Precision: This is the ratio of the number of positively classified categories that were actually found to be correctly predicted positive categories. In other words, precision is the answer to the query of how many of all patients who were predicted as positive actually have COVID-19 infection. High precision is expected.

F1 score: It is hard to compare two models that have a high recall but low precision, or a low recall but high precision. To make this comparison possible, F1-Score is typically employed. It makes it possible to measure both precision and recall simultaneously. In actuality, we use the Harmonic Mean in place of the Arithmetic Mean. As a result, we punish the extreme values even more.

AUC: The Area Under the Curve (AUC), which serves as a summary of the ROC curve, is used to gauge a classifier's ability to distinguish between classes. The greater the AUC, the superior the model does in distinguishing between the negative and positive classifications

Table 1-show formulas to calculate evaluate indices.

Table 1: Evaluation Indices formula [13]

Evaluation Indices	Calculation Formulas
Accuracy	$Acc = (TP+TN)/(TP+TN+FN+FP)$
Sensitivity	$Sen = TP/(TP+FN)$
Specificity	$Spe = TN/(FP+TN)$
Precision	$Pre = TP/(FP+TP)$
F1 Score	$F1 = (2*Pre*Sen)/(Pre+Sen)$
Dice Score	$2*TP/(TP+FP)+(TP+FN)$

7. Future Scope

The future scope for a project of COVID detection using deep learning is vast and promising.

In the future, such deep learning-based COVID detection systems can be further improved by incorporating more extensive datasets, including diverse patient demographics, medical history, and various imaging modalities. Additionally, the development of the explainable AI trchnique can help clinicians understand how the deep learning models arrive at their diagnosis, improving the trust and reliability of the system.

Overall, the future of COVID detection using deep learning is bright and continued research in this field can lead to improved diagnosis, treatment and ultimately, better outcomes for patients.

8. Experimental Results of reviewed Papers [14 - 53]

In Table 2, this table contains information on various deep learning models and their performance on various datasets. The columns include:

- Reference: the citation or source of the model
- Author: the creator of the model
- Modalities: the type of data the model was trained on (e.g. image, text, audio)
- Dataset: the specific dataset the model was trained and tested on
- Pre-processing: any pre-processing steps taken on the data before feeding it into the model
- Layers: the number and type of layers used in the model
- Activation function: the activation function used in the model
- DNN: the type of deep neural network used
- Result: the performance of the model on the dataset (e.g. accuracy, F1 score)

Table 2: Summary of Deep Learning Methodologies for Automated COVID-19 Patient Detection

Reference	Author	Modalities	dataset	Pre-processing technique	Layers	Activation function	DNN	Result
[14]	Sarra Guefrechi	X-ray	Combination of different dataset	DA and Resizing	Modified version	softmax	VGG16	Acc=98.30 Sen=98.25 Spe=98.33 Recall=98 Pre=98 F1-Score=98
[15]	Shuo Wang	CT-Scan	Clinical	DenseNet121 FPN-for Lung Segmentation, 3-Dimensional Bounding Box, Non-Lung Area Suppression Operation	4 Dense Blocks +9 layers	sigmoid	COVID-19 Net	Acc=81.24 Auc=0.90 Sen=78.93 Spe=89.93 F1-Score=86.92
[16]	Ali Narin,	X-ray	Combination of different datasets	Rescaling	Modified version	softmax	ResNet50	Acc=98 Recall=96 Spe=100
[17]	Halgurd S. Maghdid	X-ray, CT-Scan	Combination of different datasets	Cropping, resizing	Modified version	softmax	Alex Net	Acc=98 Spe=96 Sen=100
[18]	Ezz El-Din Hemdan	X-ray	Cohen's Git Hub	Rescaling	Standard version	softmax	COVIDX-Net	Acc=90 pre=83 F1-Score=91
[19]	Biraja Ghoshal	CT-Scan	Clinical	Segmentation, Rescaling, Multi-view Fusion	Modified version	Dense Layer	ResNet50	Acc=76 Spe=61.5 Sen=81.1
[20]	Linda Wang	X-ray	COVIDx	DA	87	softmax	COVID-Net	Acc=93.3 Sen=91 PPV=98.9
[21]	Xingyi Yang	CT-Scan	Combination of different dataset	Resizing, DA	Standard version	NA	DenseNet-169+	Auc=94.8 Acc=83 F1-Score=84.6

Ref						ASPP Layer	
[22]	Chuansheng Zheng,	CT-Scan	Clinical	Normalizing,Resampling,DA,3D Lung Mask Generation using 2D U-Net	20	softmax	DeCoVNet	ACC=90.8
[23]	Shaoping Hu	CT-Scan	COVID-19 Clinical Dataset/TCIA Dataset	DA, Fixed Size Sliding Window, Segmentation using U-Net	27	softmax	CNN	Acc=96.2 pre=97.3 Sen=94.5 Spe=95.3 AUC=97
[24]	Narinder Singh Punn	X-ray	Combination of different dataset	Class Balancing Methods, Binary, Thresolding, Adaptive Total variation Method	Modified version	softmax	NAS-Net Large	Acc=98 pre=88 Spe=95 F1-Score=89
[25]	Enzo Tartaglione	X-ray	6 Different Datasets	Histogram, Segmentation using U-Net, Intensity Normalization	Standard version	softmax	ResNet18	Acc=100 spec=100 Sen=100 F1-Score=100
[26]	Xiaocong Chen	CT-Scan	Combination of different dataset	Resizing, GL, DA	9 ResneXt blocks+1 4 Layers	sigmoid	Residual Attention U-Net	Acc=89 Pre=95 DSC=94
[27]	Dailin Lv	X-ray	Dataset1/Dataset2	Adaptive Histogram, CLAHE Method, MoEx,Use U-Net to Segment Lung area(VGC19),DA	Modified version	sigmoid	Cascade-SEMENet	ACC=85.6 F1-Score=86 / ACC=97.1 F1-Score=97
[28]	Mesut Toğaçar	X-ray	Combination of differnent datasets	Fuzzy colour Method, Image stacking Technique	Standard version	SMO-SVM	MobileNetV2/squeezeNet	Acc=99.27
[29]	Asif Iqbal Khan	X-ray	Combination of different dataset	Rescaling	Modified version	softmax	CoroNet	Acc=89.5 pre=97 F1-Score=98

[30]	Tulin Ozturk	X-ray	Combination of different dataset	NA	39	Linear	DarkCovidNet	Acc=98.08 Spe=95.3 Sen=95.13 Pre=98.03 F1- Score=96.51
[31]	Xiangjun Wu	CT-Scan	Clinical	Different Methods	Standard version	softmax	ResNet-101,Xception	Acc=99.02 Spe=100 Sen=98.04
[32]	Weiyi Xie	CT-Scan	COPD Dataset/COVID-19 Set	Standard pre-processing	2 RU-Net	sigmoid, softmax	RTSU-Net	IOU=92.2 ASSD=86.6
[33]	Suat Toraman	X-ray	Cohens Git Hub	DA	standard version	softmax	Capsnet	Acc=97.24 Sen=97.42 Spe=97.04 pre=97.06 F1-score=97.24
[34]	Muammer Turkoglu	X-ray	COVIDx	DA,RGB format, Normalizing	Standard version	Decision -Making System	COVIDiagnosis-Net	Acc=98.3 Spe=99.13 F1-Score=98.3
[35]	Asmaa Abbas	X-ray	combination of two datasets	histogram, DA	standard version	NA	DeTraC	Acc = 93.1
[36]	Rachna Jain	X-ray	Combination of differnent datasets	Rescaling, DA	Standard version +8	sigmoid	ResNet-18	Sen=96 Spe=70.65 AUC=95.18
[37]	Linda Wang	X-ray	COVIDx dataset	NA	standard version	softmax	COVID-Net	Acc=93.3
[38]	Amine Amyar	CT-Scan	ItalianSociety of Medical and Interentional Radiology	Resizing, Gl, Intensity Normalization	50	sigmoid	U-Net	Sen=86.7 Spe=99.3 Dice-Score=83.1
[39]	Aijaz Ahmad Reshi	X-ray	Combination of different dataset	image analysis, DA	standard version	sigmoid	NA	Acc=100 Spe=100 Sen=100 Pre=100 F1- Score=100 AUC=100

16

	Author	Modality	Dataset	Method	Version	Classifier	Model	Results
[40]	Azher Uddin	X-ray	Combination of different dataset	DA	Modified version	softmax	MobileNetV2	COVID-19 Acc=98 Pre=0.99 Recall=0.96 F1-Score=0.98 / Normal Pre=0.97 Recall=0.99 F1-Score=0.98 Acc=98
[41]	Bo Wang	CT-Scan	Clinical	Visual Data Annotation and Quality, Normalization, 3D U-Net++ for Segmentation, DA	Standard version	softmax	ResNet 50	Sen=97.4 Spe=92.2 AUC=99.1
[42]	Yu-Huan Wu	CT-Scan	COVID-CS1 Dataset	DA, Segmentation using Encoder-Decoder Model	Standard version	softmax	Res2Net	Sen=95 Spe=93 Dice Score=78.3
[43]	Aras M.Ismael	X-ray	NA	Resized, Grayscale	modified version	softmax layer	ResNet50	Acc=94.74 Sen=91 Spe=98.89 F1-score=94.79 AUC=99.9
[44]	Tej Bahadur Chandra	X-ray	Combination of different dataset	DA, Histogram, Feature Extraction using Alex Net,PCA,K-means	Standard version	softmax	DeTrac	Acc=95.12 Spe=91.87 Sen=97.91
[45]	Sarra Guefrechi	X-ray	Combination of different dataset	DA	modified version	softmax	VGG16	Acc=98.3 Sen=98.25 Spe=98.33 pre=98 Recall=98 F1-score=98
[46]	Wentao Zhao	CT-Scan	Clinical	DA	standard version	softmax	Bit-M	Acc=98 Sen=99.3 Spe=99.8 PPV=99.8 NPV=99.3

Ref	Author	Image	Dataset	Preprocessing	Version	Classifier	Model	Results
[47]	Kanij Fatema Bushra	X-ray	Cohens Git Hub	NA	Modified version	softmax	GoogleN et	Acc=98.65 Sen=98.49 Spe=98.82 pre=98.81 F1-score=98.65
[48]	Nicolas Dimeglio	X-ray	Combination of different dataset	Removes the corrupted images, cleans and normalizes	modified version	Decision tree, Random Forest, Logistic regressio n, Perceptr on, Gradient Boosting , Multi Level Perceptr on	ResNet 152	Acc=99
[49]	S Srivarsha n	X-ray	GitHub repository / Kaggle	DA	standard version	softmax	VGG	Acc=97
[50]	K. Shankar	X-ray	CXR dataset	Gaussian Filtering	standard version	softmax	BMO-CRNN	Acc=94.82 Sen=98.38 Spe=98.82 F1-score=99.03
[51]	DanielAri as-Garzón	X-ray	Combination of different dataset	lung segmentation	standard version	NA	VGG19 and U-Net	Acc=98.75 F1-Score=93.06 Recall=92.85 Pre=93.27
[52]	Jingdong Yang	X-ray	Kaggle's COVID-19 Database	Evaluation Index and DA	standard version	softmax	CodnNet	Acc=98.5 pre=98.2 Recall=97.6 F1-score=97.8 AP=99.2 AUC=99.7
[53]	Ioannis D.	X-ray	Cohen's Git GitHub	Rescaling and DA	standard version	NA	Mobile Net v2	Acc=99.18 Sen=97.36

18

Apostolo poulos				Spe=99.42

9. Chart Representation

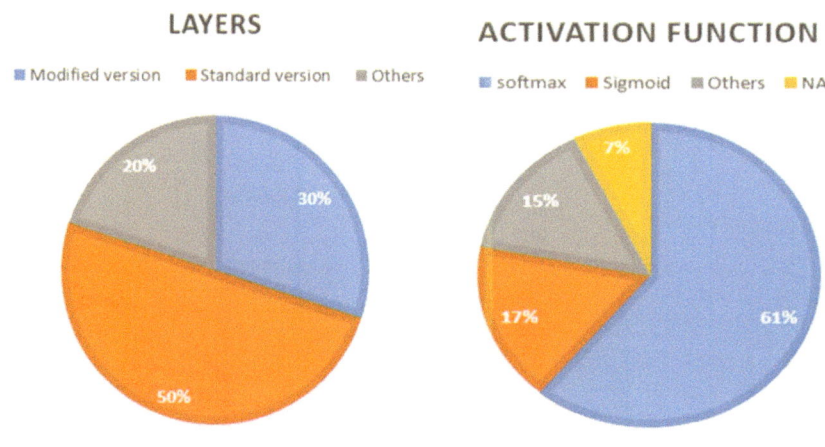

Figure 7 (a): Layers Pie chart   Figure 7 (b): Activation Function Pie chart

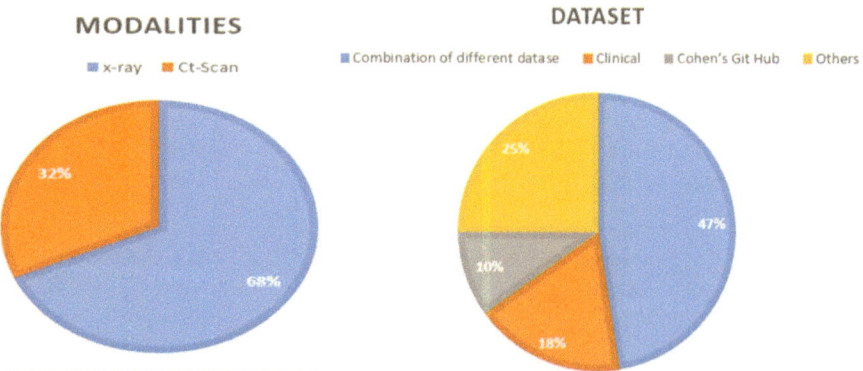

Figure 7 (c): Modalities Pie chart   Figure 7 (d): Datasets Pie chart

Figure 7(a) shows that 50% of the total falls under the category of standard, While 30% falls under modified and 20% falls under other. Figure 7(b) had four sections, with each section representing a percentage of the whole. The largest section was labelled "Softmax" and takes up 61% of the chart. The second largest section was labelled "Sigmoid" and make up 17% of the chart. The third section was labelled "Other" and takes up 15% of the chart. The smallest section was labelled "NA" and represent

7% of the chart. Overall, the chart shows majority of the data falls under the "Softmax" category, with "Sigmoid" being the second most common "Other" and "NA" make up the remaining percentages.

Figure 7(c) shows that most of the researchers preferred to use Of X-Ray images rather than CT-Scan images to train models. Figure 7(d) chart was divided into four sections representing different categories of data. The largest section, which accounts for 47% of the chart, represents a combination of various datasets. The second largest section, which accounts for 25% of the chart, was labelled "Other" and represents data that does not fit into any of the other categories. The third largest section, accounting for 18% of the chart, represents clinical data. Finally, the smallest section, representing 10% of the chart, was labelled Cohens GitHub, and represents a specific dataset related to this project.

10. Conclusion

This study uses CNN trained on datasets of chest X-ray & CT-Scan images to demonstrate the efficient and precise diagnosis of COVID-19.

This review paper used DL networks to do a thorough analysis of the completed studies of COVID-19 diagnosis. The public databases that can be used to identify and forecast COVID-19 are displayed. Tables 2 present, respectively, the cutting-edge DL methods used for the diagnosis, segmentation, and forecasting of the spread of COVID-19. I firmly believe that academics can create better DL models to reliably detect and predict the COVID19 if there are more public databases available. Thus, this will aid in creating the model that performs the best. An accurate model can be make using the features that were retrieved from the ML and DL models.

Different CNN architecture types were introduced to produce findings that were more accurate. Future generations will be motivated by this technology to resolve this undesirable state. In the future, a sizable number of CXR images from patients with SARSCoV-2 infection could be added to the dataset and training, which would be a fantastic observation. To ascertain the accuracy values and compare them in the context of accuracy, recall, precision and F1-score, other networks of CNN models can be developed.

References

1. Total no. of COVID-19 cases according to who :-https://covid19.who.int/
2. Total cases and death data available at :- https://www.worldometers.info/coronavirus/
3. X-Ray Information :- https://www.radiologyinfo.org/en/info/chestrad
4. CT-Scan image :- https://www.cureus.com/articles/39624-characteristics-of-chest-ct-images-in-patients-with-covid-19-pneumonia-in-london-uk
5. X-Ray image :- https://www.scirp.org/journal/paperinformation.aspx?paperid=108742
6. State wise COVID-19 Report :- https://www.mygov.in/corona-data/covid19-statewise-status/
7. Dataset available at :- https://www.kaggle.com/datasets/tawsifurrahman/covid19-radiography-database
8. Dataset available at :- https://www.kaggle.com/datasets/imdevskp/corona-virus-report?select=covid_19_clean_complete.csv
9. Dataset available at :- https://www.kaggle.com/datasets/nih-chest-xrays/data
10. Dataset available at :- https://github.com/ieee8023/covid-chestxray-dataset
11. Decision tree available at :- https://www.javatpoint.com/machine-learning-decision-tree-classification-algorithm
12. Confusion table:- https://www.guru99.com/confusion-matrix-machine-learning-example.html
13. Evaluation Indices formula table :-https://www.researchgate.net/publication/354196275
14. Guefrechi, Sarra, Marwa Ben Jabra, Adel Ammar, Anis Koubaa, and Habib Hamam. "Deep learning based detection of COVID-19 from chest X-ray images." *Multimedia Tools and Applications* 80, no. 21 (2021): 31803-31820.
15. Wang, Shuo, Yunfei Zha, Weimin Li, Qingxia Wu, Xiaohu Li, Meng Niu, Meiyun Wang et al. "A fully automatic deep learning system for COVID-19 diagnostic and prognostic analysis." *European Respiratory Journal* 56, no. 2 (2020).
16. Narin, Ali, Ceren Kaya, and Ziynet Pamuk. "Automatic detection of coronavirus disease (covid-19) using x-ray images and deep convolutional neural networks." *Pattern Analysis and Applications* 24, no. 3 (2021): 1207-1220.
17. Maghdid, Halgurd S., Aras T. Asaad, Kayhan Zrar Ghafoor, Ali Safaa Sadiq, Seyedali Mirjalili, and Muhammad Khurram Khan. "Diagnosing COVID-19 pneumonia from X-ray and CT images using deep learning and transfer learning algorithms." In *Multimodal image exploitation and learning 2021*, vol. 11734, pp. 99-110. SPIE, 2021.
18. Hemdan, Ezz El-Din, Marwa A. Shouman, and Mohamed Esmail Karar. "Covidx-net: A framework of deep learning classifiers to diagnose covid-19 in x-ray images." *arXiv preprint arXiv:2003.11055* (2020).
19. Ghoshal, Biraja, and Allan Tucker. "Estimating uncertainty and interpretability in deep learning for coronavirus (COVID-19) detection." *arXiv preprint arXiv:2003.10769* (2020).
20. Wang, Linda, Zhong Qiu Lin, and Alexander Wong. "Covid-net: A tailored deep convolutional neural network design for detection of covid-19 cases from chest x-ray images." *Scientific Reports* 10, no. 1 (2020): 1-12.
21. Yang, Xingyi, Xuehai He, Jinyu Zhao, Yichen Zhang, Shanghang Zhang, and Pengtao Xie. "COVID-CT-dataset: a CT scan dataset about COVID-19." *arXiv preprint arXiv:2003.13865* (2020).
22. Zheng, Chuangsheng, Xianbo Deng, Qiang Fu, Qiang Zhou, Jiapei Feng, Hui Ma, Wenyu Liu, and Xinggang Wang. "Deep learning-based detection for COVID-19 from chest CT using weak label." *MedRxiv* (2020): 2020-03.
23. Hu, Shaoping, Yuan Gao, Zhangming Niu, Yinghui Jiang, Lao Li, Xianglu Xiao, Minhao Wang et al. "Weakly supervised deep learning for covid-19 infection detection and classification from ct images." *IEEE Access* 8 (2020): 118869-118883.
24. Punn, Narinder Singh, and Sonali Agarwal. "Automated diagnosis of COVID-19 with limited posteroanterior chest X-ray images using fine-tuned deep neural networks." *Applied Intelligence* 51, no. 5 (2021): 2689-2702.
25. Tartaglione, Enzo, Carlo Alberto Barbano, Claudio Berzovini, Marco Calandri, and Marco Grangetto. "Unveiling covid-19 from chest x-ray with deep learning: a hurdles race with small data." *International Journal of Environmental Research and Public Health* 17, no. 18 (2020): 6933.

26. Chen, Xiaocong, Lina Yao, and Yu Zhang. "Residual attention u-net for automated multi-class segmentation of covid-19 chest ct images." *arXiv preprint arXiv:2004.05645* (2020).
27. Lv, Dailin, Wuteng Qi, Yunxiang Li, Lingling Sun, and Yaqi Wang. "A cascade network for detecting covid-19 using chest x-rays." *arXiv preprint arXiv:2005.01468* (2020).
28. Toğaçar, Mesut, Burhan Ergen, and Zafer Cömert. "COVID-19 detection using deep learning models to exploit Social Mimic Optimization and structured chest X-ray images using fuzzy color and stacking approaches." *Computers in biology and medicine* 121 (2020): 103805.
29. Khan, Asif Iqbal, Junaid Latief Shah, and Mohammad Mudasir Bhat. "CoroNet: A deep neural network for detection and diagnosis of COVID-19 from chest x-ray images." *Computer methods and programs in biomedicine* 196 (2020): 105581.
30. Ozturk, Tulin, Muhammed Talo, Eylul Azra Yildirim, Ulas Baran Baloglu, Ozal Yildirim, and U. Rajendra Acharya. "Automated detection of COVID-19 cases using deep neural networks with X-ray images." *Computers in biology and medicine* 121 (2020): 103792.
31. Wu, Xiangjun, Hui Hui, Meng Niu, Liang Li, Li Wang, Bingxi He, Xin Yang et al. "Deep learning-based multi-view fusion model for screening 2019 novel coronavirus pneumonia: a multicentre study." *European Journal of Radiology* 128 (2020): 109041.
32. Xie, Weiyi, Colin Jacobs, Jean-Paul Charbonnier, and Bram Van Ginneken. "Relational modeling for robust and efficient pulmonary lobe segmentation in CT scans." *IEEE transactions on medical imaging* 39, no. 8 (2020): 2664-2675.
33. Toraman, Suat, Talha Burak Alakus, and Ibrahim Turkoglu. "Convolutional capsnet: A novel artificial neural network approach to detect COVID-19 disease from X-ray images using capsule networks." *Chaos, Solitons & Fractals* 140 (2020): 110122.
34. Ucar, Ferhat, and Deniz Korkmaz. "COVIDiagnosis-Net: Deep Bayes-SqueezeNet based diagnosis of the coronavirus disease 2019 (COVID-19) from X-ray images." *Medical hypotheses* 140 (2020): 109761.
35. Abbas, Asmaa, Mohammed M. Abdelsamea, and Mohamed Medhat Gaber. "Classification of COVID-19 in chest X-ray images using DeTraC deep convolutional neural network." *Applied Intelligence* 51, no. 2 (2021): 854-864.
36. Zhang, Jianpeng, Yutong Xie, Guansong Pang, Zhibin Liao, Johan Verjans, Wenxing Li, Zongji Sun et al. "Viral pneumonia screening on chest X-rays using confidence-aware anomaly detection." *IEEE transactions on medical imaging* 40, no. 3 (2020): 879-890.
37. Wang, Linda, Zhong Qiu Lin, and Alexander Wong. "Covid-net: A tailored deep convolutional neural network design for detection of covid-19 cases from chest x-ray images." *Scientific Reports* 10, no. 1 (2020): 1-12.
38. Zhou, Tongxue, Stéphane Canu, and Su Ruan. "Automatic COVID-19 CT segmentation using U-Net integrated spatial and channel attention mechanism." *International Journal of Imaging Systems and Technology* 31, no. 1 (2021): 16-27.
39. Aijaz Ahmad Reshi, Furqan Rustam, Arif Mehmood, Abdulaziz Alhossan, Ziyad Alrabiah, Ajaz Ahmad, Hessa Alsuwailem, Gyu Sang Choi, "An Efficient CNN Model for COVID-19 Disease Detection Based on X-Ray Image Classification", *Complexity*, vol. 2021, Article ID 6621607, 12 pages, 2021. https://doi.org/10.1155/2021/6621607
40. Azher Uddin, Bayazid Talukder, Mohammad Monirujjaman Khan, Atef Zaguia, "Study on Convolutional Neural Network to Detect COVID-19 from Chest X-Rays", *Mathematical Problems in Engineering*, vol. 2021, Article ID 3366057, 11 pages, 2021. https://doi.org/10.1155/2021/3366057
41. Jin, Shuo, Bo Wang, Haibo Xu, Chuan Luo, Lai Wei, Wei Zhao, Xuexue Hou et al. "AI-assisted CT imaging analysis for COVID-19 screening: Building and deploying a medical AI system in four weeks." *MedRxiv* (2020).
42. Wu, Yu-Huan, Shang-Hua Gao, Jie Mei, Jun Xu, Deng-Ping Fan, Rong-Guo Zhang, and Ming-Ming Cheng. "Jcs: An explainable covid-19 diagnosis system by joint classification and segmentation." *IEEE Transactions on Image Processing* 30 (2021): 3113-3126.
43. Ismael, Aras M., and Abdulkadir Şengür. "Deep learning approaches for COVID-19 detection based on chest X-ray images." *Expert Systems with Applications* 164 (2021): 114054.
44. Abbas, Asmaa, Mohammed M. Abdelsamea, and Mohamed Medhat Gaber. "Classification of COVID-19 in chest X-ray images using DeTraC deep convolutional neural network." *Applied Intelligence* 51, no. 2 (2021): 854-864.

45. Guefrechi, Sarra, Marwa Ben Jabra, Adel Ammar, Anis Koubaa, and Habib Hamam. "Deep learning based detection of COVID-19 from chest X-ray images." *Multimedia Tools and Applications* 80, no. 21 (2021): 31803-31820.
46. Zhao, Wentao, Wei Jiang, and Xinguo Qiu. "Deep learning for COVID-19 detection based on CT images." *Scientific Reports* 11, no. 1 (2021): 1-12.
47. Bushra, Kanij Fatema, Md Asif Ahamed, and Mohiuddin Ahmad. "Automated detection of COVID-19 from X-ray images using CNN and Android mobile." *Research on Biomedical Engineering* 37, no. 3 (2021): 545-552.
48. Dimeglio, N., Romano, S., Vesseron, A., Pelegrin, V., Ouchani, S. (2021). COVID-DETECT: A Deep Learning Based Approach to Accelerate COVID-19 Detection. In: Bellatreche, L., Chernishev, G., Corral, A., Ouchani, S., Vain, J. (eds) Advances in Model and Data Engineering in the Digitalization Era. MEDI 2021. Communications in Computer and Information Science, vol 1481. Springer, Cham. https://doi.org/10.1007/978-3-030-87657-9_13
49. Srivarshan, S., Prithvi Seshadri, E. Kaarthikand, and A. Vijayalakshmi. "Web Based COVID Detection System using Deep Learning." In *Journal of Physics: Conference Series*, vol. 2115, no. 1, p. 012038. IOP Publishing, 2021.
50. Shankar, K., Eswaran Perumal, Vicente García Díaz, Prayag Tiwari, Deepak Gupta, Abdul Khader Jilani Saudagar, and Khan Muhammad. "An optimal cascaded recurrent neural network for intelligent COVID-19 detection using Chest X-ray images." *Applied soft computing* 113 (2021): 107878.
51. Arias-Garzón, Daniel, Jesús Alejandro Alzate-Grisales, Simon Orozco-Arias, Harold Brayan Arteaga-Arteaga, Mario Alejandro Bravo-Ortiz, Alejandro Mora-Rubio, Jose Manuel Saborit-Torres et al. "COVID-19 detection in X-ray images using convolutional neural networks." *Machine Learning with Applications* 6 (2021): 100138.
52. Yang, Jingdong, Lei Zhang, Xinjun Tang, and Man Han. "CodnNet: A lightweight CNN architecture for detection of COVID-19 infection." *Applied Soft Computing* 130 (2022): 109656.
53. Research paper :- https://arxiv.org/ftp/arxiv/papers/2004/2004.00338.pdf :1-14